Doctor Dyslexia Dude!

written by
Dr. Shawn & Inshirah Robinson

illustrated by
Brandon Hadnot

Copyright 2018 ©

Written by: Dr. Shawn Anthony Robinson & Mrs. Inshirah V. Robinson
Illustrated by Brandon Hadnot

ISBN 978-1-7323349-5-3

Library of Congress Control Number: 2018956376
First Edition 10987654321

Please visit http://drdyslexiadude.com for ordering information, updates, and scheduling a book reading event.

his book is dedicated to our sons, Jeremiah and Ezekiel. You are the light of our lives, you inspire us and remind us just how precious life is. We hope this book starts a lifelong love of reading. his book is also dedicated to Shawn's mom, Michelle Myers, who worked countless hours to make sure Shawn got the help he needed.

All rights reserved. Dr. Dyslexia Dude, its logo, and all characters are trademarks of Dr. Shawn Anthony Robinson unless otherwise noted by the authors. No part of Dr. Dyslexia Dude may be reproduced or transmitted, in any form or by any means (electronic, mechanical, photocopy) without the permission.

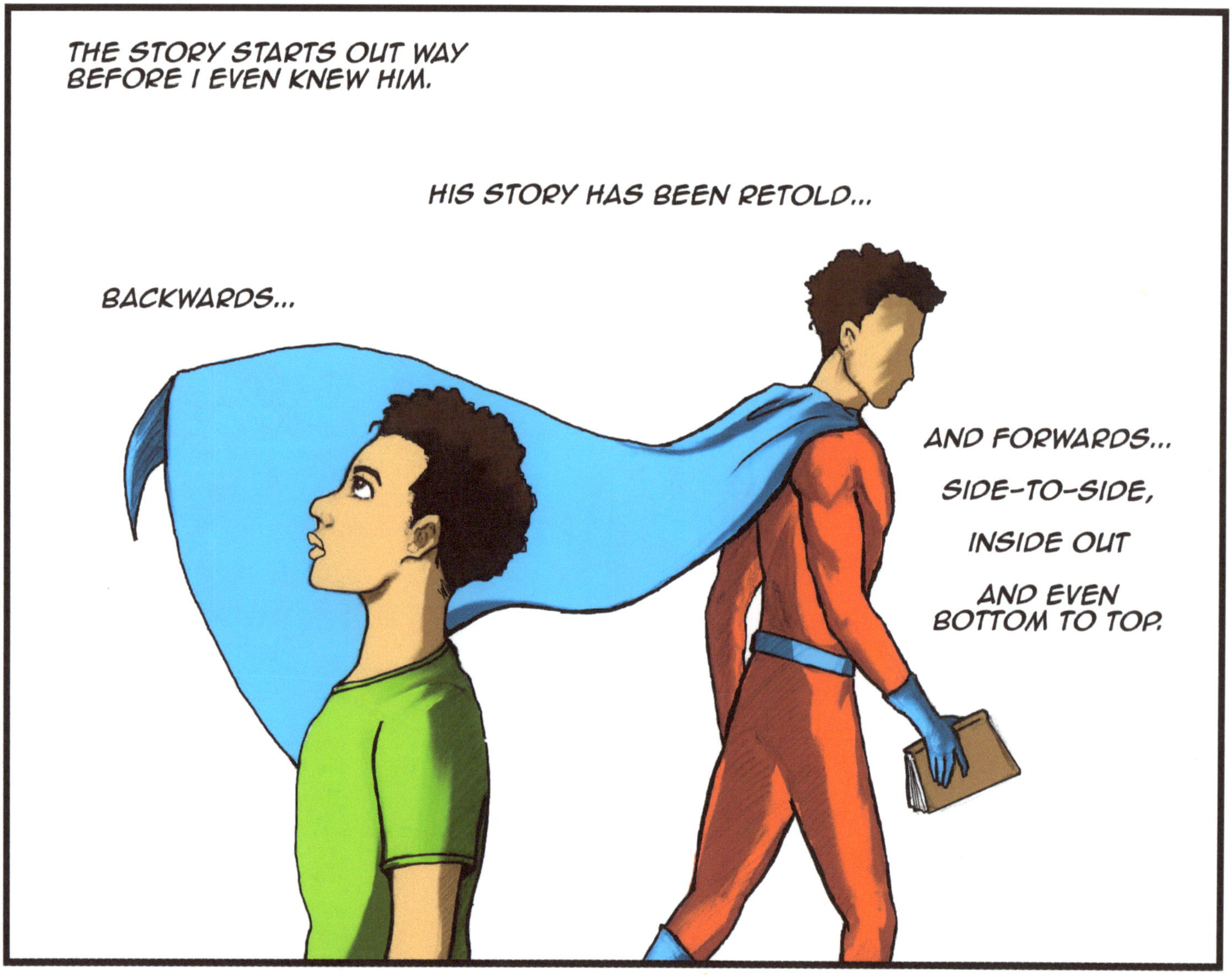

Panel 1:

THE STORY STARTS OUT WAY BEFORE I EVEN KNEW HIM.

HIS STORY HAS BEEN RETOLD...

BACKWARDS...

AND FORWARDS...

SIDE-TO-SIDE,

INSIDE OUT

AND EVEN BOTTOM TO TOP.

Panel 2:

SAD THING IS... THAT'S HOW SHAWN WOULD SEE THINGS ON THE WRITTEN PAGE.

BACKWARDS?

... BACKWARDS, LIKE WITH THE LETTERS B AND D.

WANT TO GO TO-- WAIT...

THIS IS YOUR CLASS?

UH... ACTUALLY, **NAH!**

I'M DOWN THE HALL, MAN. C'MON!

BEFORE ARRIVING INTO HIS SEVENTH-GRADE SPECIAL EDUCATION CLASSROOM, SHAWN WAS MISBEHAVING IN THE HALLWAY WITH HIS FRIEND.

ONE DAY...

WHEN HE SETTLED INTO CLASS, THE TEACHER INFORMED EVERYONE THAT THEY WOULD BE READING ALOUD FROM THE HISTORY BOOK...

YOU'RE LATE...

... AND ASSIGNED EACH STUDENT A PASSAGE.

SLAM!

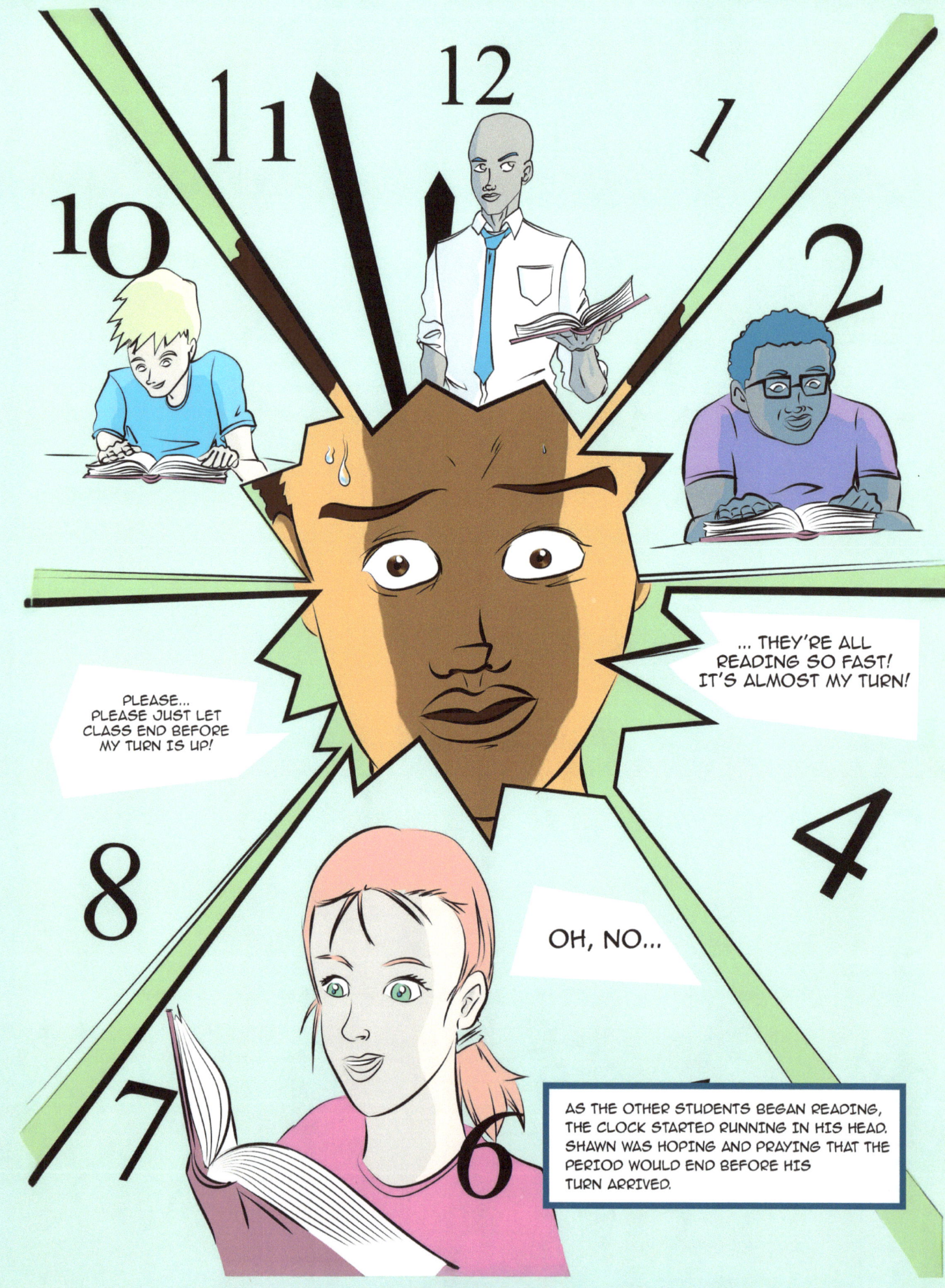

THE FIRST THREE STUDENTS HAD COMPLETED READING AND SHAWN'S BLOOD PRESSURE CONTINUED TO RISE. AS HIS TURN WAS GETTING CLOSER, ALL HE THOUGHT ABOUT WAS HIS ESCAPE. HE WANTED TO BE SAVED.

AS HIS TURN APPROACHED, SHAWN COULD NOT UNDERSTAND WHAT WAS BEING READ, AND HOW THE PASSAGES IN THE BOOK WERE LINKED. WHILE HE WAS WAITING HIS TURN SHAWN PRACTICED READING AND REREADING THE PASSAGE TO MAKE SURE HE DID NOT SOUND STUPID.

SHAWN WAS BEING ATTACKED FROM BOTH ANXIETY AND DYSLEXIA.

SHAWN!

GO TO THE OFFICE!

SHAWN HAD SAVED HIMSELF BY GETTING REMOVED FROM CLASS.

FAST FORWARD...

SHAWN'S FRUSTRATION CONTINUED...

IN HIGH SCHOOL, HE FELT HOPELESS, AND WAS IN CONSTANT TROUBLE.

NO ADULT WAS TEACHING HIM HOW TO READ.

DESPITE HIS ACADEMIC OBSTACLES, HE BECAME A PEER MENTOR WITH THE SPECIAL OLYMPICS PROGRAM.

HE WAS STILL ANGRY, AND AT THE BOTTOM OF HIS CLASS.

THE STORY OF SHAWN LEARNING TO READ IS WHEN HE MET DR. ROBERT T. NASH

Shawn would always say "The journey may be long, but stay encouraged and hopeful, and you, too, can succeed."

DR. NASH INSPIRED SHAWN TO BECOME A **SCHOLAR**.

MASTER'S DEGREE

UNDERGRADUATE DEGREE

DR. ROBERT T. NASH AND SHAWN ROBINSON

DR. SHAWN ANTHONY ROBINSON, PhD

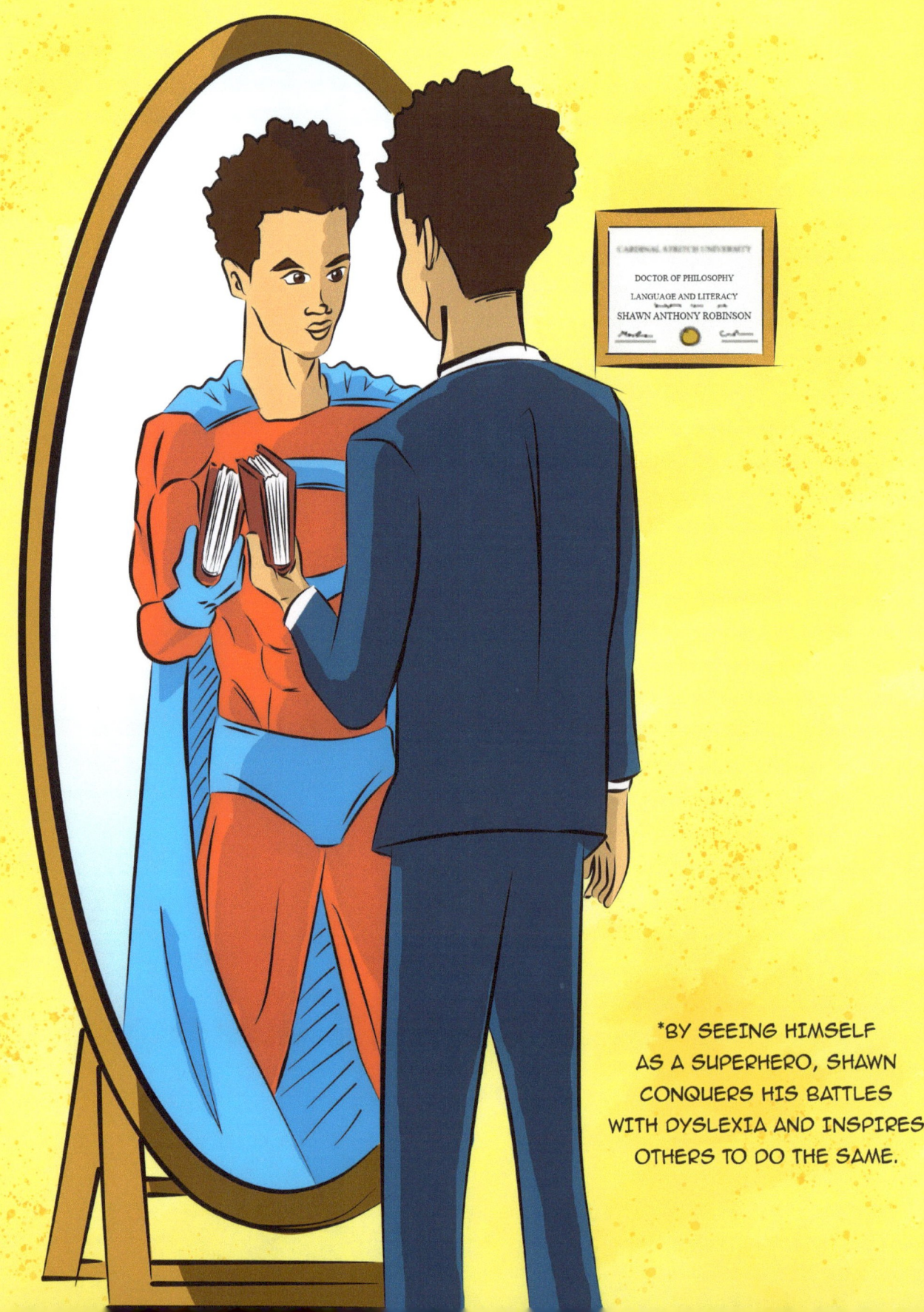

BY THE WAY, WITH ALL THE STUFF GOING ON IN HIS STORY, I FORGOT TO INTRODUCE MYSELF TO YOU.

MY NAME IS JEREMIAH, AND I DON'T JUST CALL HIM DOCTOR SHAWN ANTHONY ROBINSON DYSLEXIA DUDE...

I CALL HIM **DAD.**

BIOGRAPHY

Authors

Shawn Anthony Robinson, Ph.D.

Shawn Anthony Robinson Ph.D. is a Senior Research Associate in the Wisconsin's Equity and Inclusion Laboratory (Wei LAB) at the University of Wisconsin-Madison, an author, a dyslexia consultant, and serves on the Board of Directors with the International Dyslexia Association. Robinson graduated from the University of Wisconsin Oshkosh (UWO) with a Bachelors of Science in Human Services, a Master's in Education from DePaul University, and a PhD in Language and Literacy from Cardinal Stritch University. Robinson has received several distinguished honors throughout his early career such as: the 2017 Alumni Achievement Award/New Trier High School Alumni Hall of Honor; the 2016 Outstanding Young Alumni Award from UWO; served as a fellow for the 2015 8th Annual Asa G. Hilliard III and Barbara A. Sizemore Research Institute on African Americans and Education – American Educational Research Association; and the 2013 Achievement Gap Institute – Vanderbilt University Peabody College of Education & Human Development; and the All-State Insurance's 2005 Educator. Robinson is also a Life Member of Alpha Phi Alpha Fraternity, Inc.

Inshirah Robinson

Inshirah Robinson is a proud wife and mother of two boys, Jeremiah and Ezekiel, who are the light of her life. She is currently a graduate student in the Doctorate of Nurse Practitioner Certified Registered Nurse Anesthetist program at the University of Wisconsin Oshkosh. She holds a Bachelors of Science in Nursing Cum Laude from the University of Wisconsin – Oshkosh and a Bachelor of Business Administration, 2006 Loyola University Chicago.

Illustrator, Graphic Artist

Brandon Hadnot-Walker

Brandon Hadnot-Walker, born December 3, 1988, is a Milwaukee, WI native living in Orlando, FL as a Graphic Designer and Filmmaker. As the son of the late Theresa Hilber, who was a local Community Organizer, Small Business owner, and Designer, he is heavily influenced by the way she infused her personal passions into her work and public speeches. Since graduating with a Bachelor of Arts degree in Media Arts and Game Development at the University of Wisconsin-Whitewater in 2011, he has been an independent professional Designer for nearly a full decade. Currently, Brandon teaches Graphic Design & Web Development in a small classroom in hopes to build the next generation of Creatives who design with their hearts first. His involvement in illustrating Doctor Dyslexia Dude is rooted in his friendship and previous creative collaborations with Dr. Shawn Anthony Robinson, PhD. spanning his years in undergrad.

ENDORSEMENTS

"Doctor Dyslexia Dude is a much-needed book. This book will show all children the possibilities that they to can do great things in the world. By seeing a superhero that has overcome a challenge will allow students to see themselves and their potential as a pathway to make the world a better place. I highly endorse this book and encourage adults to get this in the hands of as many children as possible so they can know that the world is waiting on them to do great things."

Chance W. Lewis, Ph.D.
Carol Grotnes Belk Distinguished Professor of Urban Education
Director, The Urban Education Collaborative
Provost Faculty Fellow for Diversity, Inclusion and Access
UNC Charlotte Center City Campus

"For many Black boys, this story will be so familiar! Across the nation, thousands of African-American boys are being misunderstood and mislabeled everyday as 'troubled students' when they may have a Disability like dyslexia. Those mislabeled often end up in the school to prison pipeline, lives and talent lost forever. This story brings this dilemma to life and like the superhero protagonist, is destined to save lives everywhere! What a jewel!"

Dr. Joy Lawson Davis
Author of "Bright, Talented and Black: A Guide for Families of African American Gifted Students"

"An uplifting and affirming story. Doctor Dyslexia Dude overcomes his biggest challenge, showing that we all can do the same by working hard and persevering."

Steve Graham
Warner Professor of Special Education
Arizona State University

Like the Phoenix rising out of the ashes, Dr. Shawn A. Robinson introduces us to a new superhero, Dyslexia Dude! Through his super powers, he shows young people how to foreground their assets, potential, and promise. This series is sure to make a major contribution to the pantheon of children's literature. Bravo Dyslexia Dude--save the day!

Fred A. Bonner II, Ed.D.
Prairie View A&M University
Whitlowe R. Green College of Education
Professor and Endowed Chair
Chief Scientist/Executive Director
Department of Educational Leadership and Counseling

www.ingramcontent.com/pod-product-compliance
Lightning Source LLC
LaVergne TN
LVHW070612080526
838200LV00103B/349